I0520810

FOUNDATIONS

A BIBLICAL VIEW FOR ALL OF LIFE

JOSEPH BOOT

WITH NATE WRIGHT & MICHAEL THIESSEN

Ezra

CONTENT

INTRODUCTION

Christianity is not private therapy nor a weekend diversion. From the apostolic declaration that Jesus is Lord—a public claim with seismic implications in the Roman world—through the patristic defense of orthodox faith, the formation of medieval Christendom, and the magisterial reformation's recovery of Scripture's authority over church and commonwealth, Christians have confessed the Gospel as public truth. It announces the incarnate, crucified, risen, and ascended Christ who reigns over all. The Puritan vision of a godly commonwealth and the neo-Calvinist insistence of Kuyper and Bavinck that no sphere lies outside Christ's sovereignty further reveal the Gospel's cultural breadth. By contrast, reducing religion to the private and therapeutic is a modern, Enlightenment-era invention.

At the Ezra Institute, we labor to recover this reformational vision—the Gospel of the Kingdom—which summons men and women to comprehensive obedience to God's Word. *Foundations* serves this end by grounding believers in the whole counsel of God and equipping the church to think and live Christianly in every sphere of life.

This curriculum fits naturally into membership classes, discipleship cohorts, evangelistic studies, men's and women's groups, and student gatherings. Groups of eight to twelve participants cultivate the richest engagement: discussion, prayer, mutual accountability, and genuine fellowship. Seekers, new believers, and mature Christians alike can grow side by side under Scripture's guidance.

At its core, *Foundations* begins with a simple but far-reaching conviction: Christianity rests on God's own self-revelation. The truth of God—His creation and its order, humanity, sin, redemption, the church, and her mission—speaks with divine authority into every aspect of life. Doctrine naturally gives rise to worship and obedience; it shapes character, directs praise, and structures culture. As participants submit their minds and lives to Scripture, the Lord dismantles shallow, privatized religion and reorders worship and work, family and education, art and science, law and culture—bringing all things under the lordship of Christ.

May the Lord deepen your love for Christ, strengthen your confidence in His Word, and mobilize you for joyful obedience in discipling the nations—beginning with your own household and community—for His glory and your neighbor's good.

JOSEPH BOOT

PRESIDENT, EZRA INSTITUTE

LECTURERS

DR. JOSEPH BOOT

PRESIDENT, EZRA

PASTOR NATE WRIGHT

CANADIAN DIRECTOR, EZRA

DR. MICHAEL THIESSEN

US CHIEF OF OPERATIONS, EZRA

THE CULTURAL CRISIS

PREPARATION

Before watching the session, prepare your heart and mind with Scripture, prayer, and reflection.

READ & MEMORIZE

He is the image of the invisible God, the firstborn over all creation. For everything was created by Him, in heaven and on earth, the visible and the invisible, whether thrones or dominions or rulers or authorities—all things have been created through Him and for Him. He is before all things, and by Him all things hold together. He is also the head of the body, the church; He is the beginning, the firstborn from the dead, so that He might come to have first place in everything.

Colossians 1:15-18

OPTIONAL VERSE

All things were created through Him, and apart from Him not one thing was created that has been created. Life was in Him, and that life was the light of men. That light shines in the darkness, yet the darkness did not overcome it.

John 1:3-5

PRAYER FOCUS

1. Ask God to give you clarity about current cultural issues.

2. Pray that He would reveal any areas of compromise in your thinking or living.

3. Pray for courage to obey Christ in all areas of life.

4. Intercede for your church and leaders, asking that they would not conform to secular culture but to Christ.

PROBING QUESTIONS

1. What do I think the Gospel is mainly about?

2. How would I currently define the word "culture"?

3. When I think of the phrase "Christ is Lord," what areas of life come to mind?

As you watch the video in session one, you can follow along and fill in the blanks.

1. THE OPENING

A. What does Scripture say about Christ as the Word?

"All things were made _____ Him, and without Him, _____ was made that was made." (John 1:3 NKJV)

B. Who is transforming whom today?

☐ The church is transforming culture

☐ Culture is transforming the church

☐ Neither

☐ Both

C. What does Paul say the Gospel concerns?

The gospel concerns _____ things.

D. What is at stake if we misunderstand this truth?

_____

_____

2. THE NEED FOR STRUCTURE

A. In both city and countryside, how is God's order visible?

- Urban: Streets, _____, people working, _____, and building.

- Rural: Farmers _____ and _____ with knowledge and precision.

B. What does this observable structure tell us about God?

☐ He prefers chaos

☐ He designed things to work without us

☐ He is a God of order and purpose

3. RECOGNIZING THE CRISIS

A. Three words describing our current moment:

"Moral, _____, and _____ upheaval."

B. How do many Christians feel today?

Many feel _____, _____, and unsure how to respond.

C. Why is it hard to name what's happening?

☐ We lack historical knowledge

☐ We're afraid of being offensive

☐ We often don't have a biblical framework for understanding culture

4. THE GOSPEL IS COSMIC IN SCOPE

A. According to Colossians 1, Christ created and holds together _____.

B. Paul says God reconciles not just some things, but _____ things through Christ.

C. The Gospel reverses the curse of sin _____ it has touched.

D. We are commanded to preach the Gospel to all _____.

E. The "map" analogy teaches that if we don't see the big picture...

☐ We'll miss church

☐ We won't understand how to navigate the world

5. RELIGION, FIRST PRINCIPLES, AND SOCIETY

A. The word "religion" means to _____ or _____ together.

B. Biblically, religion is rooted in the _____, which is the center of man.

C. G.K. Chesterton said that abandoning first principles leads to _____.

D. Nietzsche's rejection of God led to _____—a picture of today's culture.

6. THE RISE OF RADICAL AUTONOMY

A. Radical autonomy = the belief that we belong to _____ and define truth on our _____ _____.

B. What has been replaced as our cultural foundation?

☐ The Bible

☐ Reason

☐ God's vertical authority has been replaced with horizontal human contracts

C. List 3 examples of issues stemming from radical autonomy:

_____

_____

_____

7. COMPROMISE IN THE CHURCH

A. Many churches today prioritize _____ _____ over biblical faithfulness.

B. Popular slogans used to justify compromise include:

- "God is a God of _____, not judgment."

- "Don't be a _____."

- "Judge not, or you will be _____."

8. GOD'S LAW & THE GOSPEL

A. Sin is defined as _____—breaking God's law.

B. Satan is referred to as the _____ _____ in 2 Thessalonians.

C. Paul says the law is for the _____ and the rebellious (1 Tim 1).

D. The Gospel and the law are not enemies, but a _____ garment.

E. Why is it dangerous to separate Gospel grace from Gospel obedience?

_____

_____

9. DISCUSSION QUESTIONS

With your group, discuss the following questions.

1. Is the idea that Jesus is Lord over all creation and every aspect of life and human societies a new idea for you, or is this something you have fully embraced?

_____

_____

2. Do you believe that most people who confess to be a Christian embrace the idea that Jesus is Lord of everything?

_____

_____

3. Why is it dangerous to shrink the Gospel to just personal salvation?

_____

_____

4. Fill in the blank: If the Gospel is just about me going to heaven, then I might ignore...

☐　How I live at work

☐　My views on politics or education

☐　My family life

☐　All of the above

5. Write a sentence describing the Gospel as more than just salvation:

_____

_____

6. What are some signs you see in society that confirm it is in moral, cultural, and ethical upheaval? Where do you see "madness" in society?

_____

_____

7. What cultural principles have replaced God's Word in the public square?

_____

_____

8. If Jesus is Lord of all, creation, life, society, government, culture, etc. why are we not witnessing his supremacy of Christ in all aspects of our society today?

_____

_____

9. When you think of the phrase "Christ is Lord," what areas of life come to mind? What areas didn't come to mind until listening to the video?

10. Joe talked about vertical accountability versus horizontal relativity—try to put that concept in your own words.

11. Where have you seen horizontal relativity override vertical accountability in society?

12. What is the danger of defining morality by consent alone?

13. Where are you personally being pressured to conform?

14. Who in your life hands you ultimatums if you don't align with their convictions?

15. Who actually shapes the way you see issues, is it Christ's Word—or someone else's word?

_____

_____

16. How does Col 1:15-23 teach that the Gospel is more than personal salvation?

_____

_____

17. Was there a new idea that came out of this session that you found very compelling, or alternatively, that you are struggling with?

_____

_____

LIVE IT OUT THIS WEEK

- Identify one area of life that you've kept separate from Christ's Lordship:

_____

_____

- Surrender it to Christ in prayer and action.

- Share what you're learning with a friend or family member.

- Memorize Colossians 1:15–18 this week.

- Ask your pastor how your church is engaging with culture biblically.

SESSION TWO

THE RELIGIOUS ROOTS OF CULTURE

PREPARATION

Before watching the session, prepare your heart and mind with Scripture, prayer, and reflection.

READ & MEMORIZE

Therefore, brothers, by the mercies of God, I urge you to present your bodies as a living sacrifice, holy and pleasing to God; this is your spiritual worship. Do not be conformed to this age, but be transformed by the renewing of your mind, so that you may discern what is the good, pleasing, and perfect will of God.

Romans 12:1-2

OPTIONAL VERSE

I am not praying that You take them out of the world but that You protect them from the evil one. They are not of the world, as I am not of the world. Sanctify them by the truth; Your word is truth. As You sent Me into the world, I also have sent them into the world.

John 17:15-18

PRAYER FOCUS

1. Ask God to reveal how certain cultures are shaping your thinking more than His Word.

2. Pray that you would live faithfully under Christ's lordship in all areas of life.

3. Intercede for Christian leaders to boldly shape political culture with the Gospel.

PROBING QUESTIONS

1. In what ways do I assume culture is neutral?

_____

_____

2. Where in my life has culture shaped me more than Christ's Word? Where does Satan have a foothold in my thinking and living?

_____

_____

As you watch the video in session two, you can follow along and fill in the blanks.

15

1. WELCOME & INTRODUCTION

A. What foundational truth is at the heart of this session? Culture is not neutral. It is the external expression of our deepest _____.

2. DEFINING CULTURE BIBLICALLY

A. Fill in the blanks:

- The word "culture" comes from the Latin word meaning the cutting edge of a _____.

- "Colonus" means to _____.

- "Cultus" means _____.

B. Culture is always shaped by a society's _____, whether explicitly or implicitly.

C. Diversity in culture reflects diversity in what people _____.

3. OBSERVING CULTURE AROUND THE WORLD

A. Culture is expressed in what areas of life? (Check all that apply)

☐ Law

☐ Education

☐ Diet

☐ Dress

☐ Art

☐ Architecture

B. In the West today, what kind of culture dominates?

☐ Christian

☐ Islamic

☐ Hindu

☐ Humanistic/Secular

4. CULTURE AS WORSHIP IN ACTION

A. Culture is not optional. All people are culture-makers, because we are made in the image of a God we _____.

B. Creation becomes culture when humans…

- Take grapes and make _____.

- Take trees and build _____.

- Use words to form _____.

- Express sexual identity through _____.

C. Where have you seen the illusion of neutrality pushed in cultural conversations?

_____

_____

5. STRUCTURE & DIRECTION

A. Match the term with its meaning (draw a line to connect):

Term	Direction
Structure	The spiritual trajectory of an action or institution
Direction	God's design or order for something

Examples:

Marriage

- **Structure:** A lifelong covenant between one man and one woman

- **Direction:**

  - *In rebellion:* selfishness, manipulation, divorce, polygamy, or same-sex unions

- *In obedience:* mutual love and respect, sacrificial leadership by the husband, willing submission by the wife, raising children in the fear and admonition of the Lord

Music

- Both Bach and Lady Gaga use the same musical _____, but their songs go in radically different moral _____.

6. NO NEUTRAL GROUND

A. Paul teaches in Romans 1 that people "exchange the _____ of God for a _____".

B. This leads to a _____ exchange, which leads to _____ _____.

C. Which is true:

☐ Culture is neutral

☐ Culture can be good or bad depending on how it's used

☐ Culture is always going in a direction—toward or away from Christ

7. REDIRECTING CULTURE

A. We are not simply to react to culture. We are to _____ it for the glory of God.

B. Christians are called to "make culture" in obedience to God by building _____, _____, and _____ that glorify Christ.

C. The fall affected every area of life, but the Gospel is God's means of _____ and _____ culture toward Him.

8. SOCIETAL BREAKDOWN = A RELIGIOUS CRISIS

A. Every cultural collapse begins with a change of _____.

B. List two current examples where cultural decline reflects a spiritual problem:

- _____

- _____

9. DISCUSSION QUESTIONS

With your group, discuss the following questions.

1. What does it mean that culture is "religion externalized"?

2. What are some different cultures you have experienced and how did they reflect their religious foundations and their belief systems?

3. Give one example of a culture you've seen shaped by a religion other than Christianity:

4. What are the ways that we have already been secularized?

5. In what areas of life (education, politics, work, entertainment, family life) do you see Christians adopting secular patterns of thought without realizing it?

6. How does this secularization lead people to depend more on their own reason than the Lord's wisdom?

7. What does Proverbs 3:5 say about this issue?

8. Do you see how impactful this really is? Do you see how it might actually lead people completely astray from God's intentions? What would be the scriptural metaphor for this divide?

9. Joe argues that, essentially, there is no neutral direction for the structure and for those who participate in a structure. Why can there be no neutral direction?

10. Where have you seen the illusion of neutrality pushed in cultural conversations?

11. Why isn't it enough to just avoid culture altogether?

12. If Christ is not shaping our culture, who is? What would you say are the main influences upon our western culture today?

13. Exercise: Think about a group or organization you're familiar with—this could be something like a t-ball league, a book club, a sports team, or even a fire hall crew.

Use the space below to reflect on the culture of that group. Culture is often described as "religion externalized"—the lived-out values, priorities, and beliefs of a community.

Consider and write down:

- What kind of language does the group use?

- How does it plan and schedule its meetings or events?

- How are members taught or trained?

- What kinds of outcomes or achievements are celebrated?

- What are the formal or informal rules everyone follows?

- How does the group manage itself and promote its activities?

Once you've written your observations, reflect on this:

- Do these cultural traits align with God's Word and the Ten Commandments?
- Are there aspects that honor God? Are there any that might offend Him?

Be ready to discuss your thoughts with the group.

---

14. How would your life look different if we truly believed that every cultural action is a form of worship?

LIVE IT OUT THIS WEEK

A. Identify one cultural habit for each structure in your life that needs to be redirected toward Christ. Make sure you address lawless habits:

Personal Habits: _____

Family Habits: _____

Neighborhood Habits: _____

Work Habits: _____

Church Habits: _____

Media Habits: _____

Political Habits: _____

Educational Habits: _____

Medical Habits: _____

- Pray for the Holy Spirit to guide you in becoming a faithful culture-maker in your community.

- Find one way this week to actively apply your faith in a cultural space (workplace, school, media, etc.).

- Ask someone you trust: "How do you see me being influenced by culture more than by Christ?"

JOURNAL PROMPT

B. How does Christ's Lordship change the way I...

Parent? _____

Vote? _____

Spend money? _____

Use media? _____

C. How can I shape my family's culture to reflect Christ's Lordship more clearly?

_____

_____

TRANSFORMING CULTURE FOR CHRIST

PREPARATION

Before watching the session, prepare your heart and mind with Scripture, prayer, and reflection.

READ & MEMORIZE

So now, kings, be wise; receive instruction, you judges of the earth. Serve the Lord with reverential awe and rejoice with trembling. Pay homage to the Son or He will be angry, and you will perish in your rebellion, for His anger may ignite at any moment. All those who take refuge in Him are happy.

Psalm 2:10-12

OPTIONAL VERSE

So that at the name of Jesus every knee will bow—of those who are in heaven and on earth and under the earth—and every tongue should confess that Jesus Christ is Lord, to the glory of God the Father.

Philippians 2:10-11

PRAYER FOCUS

1. Pray that your faith would move beyond theory and into obedient action.

2. Ask God to use your daily work and life for Kingdom transformation.

3. Intercede for government leaders to turn from self-rule to Christ's lordship.

PROBING QUESTIONS

1. Have I treated the Gospel as only personal salvation? If so, how?

_____

_____

2. Where do I see my own vocation as part of shaping culture for Christ?

_____

_____

3. What do I think "faithful cultural engagement" actually looks like in my vocation?

_____

_____

As you watch the video in session three, you can follow along and fill in the blanks.

1. FROM WORSHIP TO CULTURE

A. Fill in the blanks:

- If culture is the public expression of _____, then the Gospel must lead to true _____.
- This true culture is described in scripture as the _____ of God.

B. Which is true:

☐ The Gospel affects our culture as much as it affects our souls.

☐ Christians were made to shape the world, not escape from it.

2. RETREAT OR REFORM

A. Why has the church lost cultural influence?

- We've retreated into a bubble of private _____.
- We've limited Christ's jurisdiction to just the _____.
- We've ignored areas like education, law, medicine, and _____.

B. What happens when we retreat?

_____

_____

3. BIBLICAL MODELS OF ENGAGEMENT

A. Match the servant of God with their act of cultural engagement (draw a line to connect):

Term	Direction
Moses	Refused to stop praying; shaped pagan court
Nathan	Confronted Pharaoh as a false god
Daniel	Preached Christ to political rulers
John the Baptist	Rebuked David for adultery
Paul	Confronted Herod about marriage

B. What do all these examples teach us?

- God expects His people to _____ sin and proclaim His _____ in public life.

4. A KINGDOM THAT CONFRONTS

A. Fill in the blanks:

- Jesus reminded Pilate: "You would have no _____ ...unless it had been given you from above." (John 19:11)

- God commands kings to "kiss the _____" (Psalm 2).

B. What does this mean?

C. Which is true:

- ☐ Christ's Lordship depends on human approval.
- ☐ God holds rulers accountable to His standard.
- ☐ We can be neutral toward Christ in politics or culture.

5. TWO CULTURAL DIRECTIONS

A. According to Joe Boot, there are only two cultural options:

- Worship of the _____

- Worship of the _____

B. Give a modern example of creature-worship in culture:

_____

C. How does Chesterton describe this danger?

"Abolish God and the _____ becomes god."

DISCUSSION QUESTIONS

1. What stood out for you most of all in this last session?

_____

_____

2. Joe repeated an important point at the start of the session, and it is worth repeating.

1. Culture is the public expression of the worship of a people.

2. The Gospel restores man to true worship.

3. Therefore the Gospel restores man to true culture.

What does the word "true" mean here? In other words, "true culture" is what kind of culture?

_____

_____

3. As stated during the video, Jesus reminded Pilate:

"You would have no _____...unless it had been given you from above." (John 19:11) And God commands kings to "kiss the _____" (Psalm 2). Now add, "All _____ has been given to me in heaven and on earth. Go, therefore, and make disciples of all nations, baptizing them in the name of the Father and of the Son and of the Holy Spirit, teaching them to observe everything I have commanded you. And remember, _____ always, to the end of the age." (Matthew 28:18-20)

What does this mean? How should it affect every conversation and every decision of our lives?

_____

_____

4. What did Joe mean when he said we have ecclesiasticized the Bible?

_____

_____

5. Joe also reminds us that when we limit the authority of scripture the result is the marginalization of the Christian Church and its influence upon our culture. Can you think of historical examples of past Christian culture making that stand in contrast to today's retreat?

_____

_____

6. What are some cultural structures that you are involved with (marriage, family, business, sports, music, art, science, education, government etc.) and how are you influencing their direction?

_____

_____

7. Where do you see idolatry occurring within these structures today?

8. What fears do you have when you think about bringing God's Word to bear in your sphere of influence? What do you assume is at stake? And who are your main opponents? In other words, who do you struggle to fear instead of fearing the Lord?

9. What steps can you take to bring God's Word to bear in your sphere of influence?

10. Which private area of your life do you most struggle to bring under Christ's rule?

11. It was argued that all Christians are called to confront sin, expose idolatry and proclaim truth, but we are to do it with Truth and Grace. How do we ensure that we are not compromising either Truth or Grace?

LIVE IT OUT THIS WEEK

- Identify one idol in your personal or local culture that needs to be challenged:

- Take one small step this week to confront it with grace and truth.

- Reflect on what faithful cultural obedience looks like in your job, home, or civic life.

- Pray Psalm 2 over your local leaders.

JOURNAL PROMPT

What would change in my daily habits if I truly believed Christ is King over my city, school, workplace, and nation?

Where have I been tempted to stay silent rather than speak God's truth into public life?

PREPARING FOR WHAT'S NEXT

This was the final session in the "Foundations" series. But Kingdom work continues.

Final Questions to Consider:

- Where has God placed me to make an impact?

- What issue has He burdened me to speak into?

- Am I more afraid of man's rejection or God's command?

Optional Reading

- Jeremiah 29:4–9

- Matthew 28:18–20

- Romans 13:1–7

Visit: www.ezrainstitute.com for more tools, resources, and training opportunities.